The New Negro

of

the South

A Portrait of Movements and Leadership

by

Wilmoth A. Carter

Director, Division of Social Science
Shaw University

An Exposition–University Book

Exposition Press New York

EXPOSITION PRESS INC.

386 Park Avenue South   New York, N.Y. 10016

FIRST EDITION

Manufactured in the United States of America

Library of Congress Catalog Card No. 67-24259

EP 45756

Contents

THE NEW NEGRO OF THE SOUTH

THE NEW NEGRO OF THE SOUTH

PART ONE

Who Is the New Negro?

One who is familiar with the numerous publications of the 1960's dealing with the Negro cannot help but be cognizant of the varied portraits of the Negro as a "New Negro." Whether viewed psychologically or sociologically, this new racial person is most often portrayed as a militant, bourgeois, social-action participant in search of self-identity, human dignity, and status equal to that of other Americans. So far removed is the new "ideal-type" Negro from the old in his portrayed de-emphasis on race and his re-emphasis on citizenship rights as an American that the designation Negro American is tending to replace the former label of American Negro. However, this is not a new designation, for Alain Locke used it casually in 1925 in *The New Negro*, while James Weldon Johnson used it emphatically in 1934 with his *Negro Americans, what now?* but it was never before so widely used as today. Observations such as these prompt us to question whether or not the New Negro is a newly emerging type of person, or if the concept is just euphemistic neologism for a long existent social type.

How new is the New Negro? Just what is involved in his acclaimed newness? Is the New Negro of the South different from the New Negro in other regions? Does he really exist outside the confines of the South? Answers to questions such as these must be sought through historically evident features of the demands, leadership, movements, and social-action programs of Negroes.

Direct-action forms of protest are often taken as evidence of the emergence of a New Negro, but the Negro discovered nonviolent direct action long before the Montgomery bus boycott of 1955, or the sit-ins of 1960. Tactics which marked the

1960 protests—sit-ins, ride-ins, picketing, etc.—had been used individually and collectively from post–Civil War days on. The essential difference is that prior to 1960 they were highly localized, and often individual, whereas in the 1960's they became generalized and collectivized. Before the 1955–60 period, such tactics had not been so extensively used by Negroes, and were certainly not accepted as a basic philosophy requiring training and discipline to effect. But then, no previous phase of the movement was so widely dispersed, so all-inclusive, and so continuously operative. When protest and direct action are viewed within the civil rights movement, the aims, goals, ideology and methods, as well as recognized leadership, are actually more different in degree than kind. Leafing through the pages of history, for example, one finds that Negroes have always "spoken out" or "acted out" in protest against racial injustices. The partial listing of incidents of protest given below is illustrative of many forms of direct action in which Negroes have engaged since the Civil War. It is worthy of note that the precedent for forms of direct action used in the 1960's had been well established before that period.

INCIDENTS OF PROTEST

Year

1867 Assault upon segregated streetcars of Philadelphia, Pennsylvania.

1871 "Ride-in" campaign in Louisville, Kentucky, which ended only when mixed seating was permitted on streetcars.

1906 Mary Church Terrell sought to directly protest against President Roosevelt's dishonorable discharge of three companies of Negro soldiers following the Brownsville, Texas, riot. She went to see the Secretary of War about the situation (the President was in Panama), and when told that he could not see her, she replied, "I'll wait anyway," which she did, until he finally saw her.[1]

1906   One hundred men and women, gathered at Harper's Ferry, West Virginia, for the second meeting of the Niagara group, marched in solemn procession to the fort where John Brown had made his stand. They vowed that August morning to dedicate themselves "to the final emancipation of the race which John Brown died to make free."[2]

1914   Trotter Incident: Delegation of Negroes went to the White House to protest segregation in government departments.[3]

1916   Negroes of Atlanta, Georgia, protested the school board's planned proposal to save enough money to build a new high school for whites by eliminating the seventh grade from colored grammar schools. Although resentful of the protest, the board decided instead to float a bond issue to secure the money. Negroes put on a house-to-house campaign to get enough Negroes registered to vote to defeat the bond issue. (Passage required two-thirds of the registered, not active, voters).[4]

1918   Defeat of the bond issue in Atlanta, Georgia, brought on a vigorous campaign by the *Atlanta Georgian*. Negroes retaliated by boycotting the paper: cancelled all subscriptions; refused to buy the paper from the stands; returned all copies delivered free.[5]

1918   Five thousand Negroes marched in silent parade in New York City, July 28, in protest against injustice, carrying banners against lynch law, segregation, race riots, etc.[6]

---

[1] Dorothy Sterling and Benjamin Quarles, *Lift Every Voice*, pp. 67–68.
[2] *Ibid.*
[3] *Negro Year Book*, 1916–17.
[4] Walter White, *A Man Called White*, pp. 29–37.
[5] *Ibid.*
[6] *Negro Year Book*, 1918–19.

1919   Colored delegates refused to eat at table in separate room at the Annual Luncheon of the State Convention of the American Legion. All walked out and purchased lunch elsewhere. (*Afro-American*, Baltimore, Oct. 10).[7]

1919   Refusal of colored residents to send their children to the separate Negro school (Pittsburgh, Pa.) forced the school to close. (*The Guardian*, Boston, Sept. 13).[8]

1919   Returned colored soldiers of St. Joseph, Missouri, refused to be hung on to the tail end of a victory parade. . . . The colored band refused to play during the parade on account of the affront to the race. (Wichita Protest).[9]

1921   NAACP Conference, Detroit, Michigan: Silent marching of 4,000 men and women, 250 autos, 6 bands on Sunday afternoon in August.

   a) Groups of eleven carried banners protesting race prejudice, etc.

   b) Groups of seven carried banners protesting payment of higher wages to those doing same work as Negroes, color-caste in labor, violence in voting, double standard in courts, etc.

   c) Groups of three carried banners protesting child labor, KKK, White Supremacy advocates, failure to name Negroes to West Point, etc.[10]

1942   Bayard Rustin engaged in one-man sit-ins at restaurants, on buses, at the beach, in taxi-driveway, etc.[11]

1947   Delegates to NAACP Youth Conference picketed Texas State University for Negroes in Houston.

1948   Group of Negro ministers marched on Capitol Hill and

---

[7] Robert T. Kerlin, *The Voice of the Negro*.
[8] *Ibid.*
[9] *Ibid.*
[10] *Crisis*, August, 1921.
[11] Jackson Toby, *Contemporary Society*, pp. 556–561.

prayed for Congress—urging legislation insuring equality in education, work, and protection under the law.[12]

1948 St. Louis, Missouri, NAACP picketed City Hall in protest against the mayor's refusal to discuss with them the appointment of a Negro to the local board of education.[13]

1948 Picketing of the Jim Crow summer-school course in education for colored teachers set up by the University of Maryland at the Negro High School in Baltimore.[14]

1948 Marked the third year of picketing by the Baltimore NAACP in protest against racial segregation at Ford's theater.[15]

1949 Five colleges demonstrated in the gallery of the Texas Senate (April 27) protesting segregation in education in Texas.[16]

1951 Mary Church Terrell instituted suit against a Thompson Restaurant, Washington, D.C., testing violation of an eighty-year-old law. While the case was being tried in the courts, she spearheaded a committee that set out to persuade five-and-ten-cent stores to open their lunch counters to Negroes. When reasoned arguments with the store managers failed, she started sit-ins and picket lines against them. The court's decision, rendered June 8, 1953, opened restaurants to Negroes in Washington for the first time since Woodrow Wilson days.[17]

1955 Montgomery bus boycott started in December, lasted a year.

1958 Sit-in by Oklahoma City, Oklahoma, NAACP Youth

[12] *Crisis*, March, 1948.
[13] *Crisis*, October, 1948.
[14] *Ibid.*
[15] *Crisis*, November, 1948.
[16] *Crisis*, June, 1949.
[17] Sterling and Quarles, *op. cit.*, p. 80.

Chapter, led by a woman teacher, resulted in desegregation of many motels, hotels, restaurants, etc.

1960 Sit-ins began in North Carolina.

1961 Freedom Rides.

1963 March on Washington held on August 28.

1965 Selma, Montgomery, march (March 25).

* * *

Violent direct action had been tried as early as 1526, with the insurrection of Negro slaves in Allyons's Colony, on the coast of what is now South Carolina,[18] but Negroes soon learned that direct action in the form of violence would defeat their purpose. Insurrections were planned continuously up to 1859, when John Brown's Raid on Harper's Ferry marked the last attempted slave insurrection. And, of course, with each attempted insurrection, the society passed laws designed to prevent recurrence of similar events. One of the end results of such laws, included among which was the Fugitive Slave Act of 1850, was to so intimidate large numbers of Negroes as to make them hesitant about protesting and demonstrating, even in their own behalf. It is this reluctance and hesitancy, formed largely as a result of legal proscriptions, that has often been mistaken for satisfaction and complacency.

The expressed wants of Negroes have likewise varied little through time. Demands for justice, political equality, equal education, and industrial and social freedom were as prevalent in the pleas of the national conventional movement, which began in 1817 and continued intermittently until the Reconstruction Era, as they are today. Even today's oft-heard cry for "Freedom Now" is merely a reecho of the Negro's consistent search for freedom and equality. It was repeatedly voiced in the Frederick Douglass declarations of the 1850's, which said: "We want full equality now."

---

[18] *Negro Year Book*, 1916–17.

The same declaration has been given all through the twentieth century. Speaking for the Negro, Dr. Emmett J. Scott wrote in the *Atlanta Post*, 1919:

> The Negro wants justice in the courts, the privilege of serving on juries, the right to vote, to hold office, better educational facilities, abolition of the "Jim Crow" car and of discrimination and segregation in government service, the same military training and chance for promotion in the army that white men enjoy, equal wages, better housing . . . and reform in Southern penal institutions.[19]

There is little difference between the declarations of the 1850's and those of 1919. Nothing new was added even in the 1940's, when the Negro's desire for first-class citizenship was made synonymous with the Rooseveltian "Four Freedoms." To translate this into action, A. Philip Randolph suggested that the task of the Negro must be to complete the bourgeois, democratic, socio-economic, political revolution in freedom, equality, and justice as set forth in the basic guiding principles of 1776, 1812, and 1865.[20]

Rifts within the civil rights movement are directly attributable to dissension among the leaders over basic goals and ways of achieving them, but this, too, must be seen as a perpetual feature and not a new one. In 1843, when Henry Highland Garnett was urging Negroes, including slaves, to strike for their lives and liberty, Frederick Douglass was advocating principles of nonresistance and moral suasion. Douglass later recognized the futility of relying on such tactics to end slavery and in the late 1850's not only became a leading exponent of "militant abolitionism" but advocated political action as a means of securing freedom. His practical implementation of this advocacy was evidenced in his leading the movement against segregated schools in Rochester, Massachusetts, and his becoming superintendent of the underground railroad there. During this same

---

[19] Kerlin, *op. cit.*, p. 51.
[20] Rayford W. Logan, ed., *What the Negro Wants*, p. 139.

period, campaigns were being conducted in varied Northern cities to end separate schools for Negroes.

The fact that the majority of protest actions of the Negro prior to the Civil War occurred in border states and Northern cities probably explains why an apparent pattern of equality seemed to emerge in these localities rather early. In each instance, however, it must be noted that direct action tended to aid in creating the new patterns. This distinguishing feature was evidenced in the often individualized and localized efforts, which yet were uttered or attempted in the interest of all Negroes. Even when considering the Negro convention movement as a whole, it must be recalled that the movement was composed of local auxiliaries which met in varied towns and cities, usually coming together for an annual meeting to adopt programs for elevating the Negro. The first truly national convention functioned as a protest organ and a communications medium through which thinking about the Negro and his demands might be centralized. It brought realization of the need for a nationally integrated program and helped unify an otherwise disparate group. Included in the Negro convention movement activities were the following: providing funds, loans, teachers, social workers, jobs and markets for goods in local communities of the North; emphasizing the importance of education; stressing courage and self-reliance; opposing emigration as a solution to problems; and exposing merchants and industrialists who refused to hire Negro help or insisted on placing Negroes only as porters.[21] Thus was the foundation laid early for a movement whose ties have stretched into the 1960's.

Controversy among Negro leaders today over the basic issues around which protest should be developed is not without its precedent either. What came to be a major issue in the Du Bois-Washington controversy in the early part of the twentieth century had been argued by the Negro convention movement in the nineteenth century. Except for opposition and weakening

---

[21] Philip S. Foner, *Life and Writings of Frederick Douglass*, Vol. II, pp. 37-38.

support—financial, personal, and ideological—what resulted in the Tuskegee Idea might have been the New Haven Idea. When debate developed over establishing a manual-labor college for Negro youth, the idea for which dates back to 1827, Douglass opposed such an institution, for he viewed it as a mechanism for perpetuating color prejudice and segregation. By 1853, he had changed his views and worked to help make the institution a reality, but opposition by many Yale professors, Yale students, and townspeople of New Haven forced abandonment of the idea of establishing such a school in New Haven. Other setbacks brought an end to the subsequent venture to disregard sex and color and erect an "American Industrial School" near Erie, Pennsylvania.[22]

Since the status of most Negroes in America was that of slave prior to 1865, perhaps one gets better historical perspective on the emergence of what is called the New Negro by considering the period following the Civil War. If perceptions of the Negro are gained from literary depictions, it is readily understandable that the Negro might be viewed today, a century after the Civil War, as being of a different ilk from the Negro of a century ago, a half century ago, or even of a decade ago. During these earlier periods, the Southern Negro was most frequently depicted as being docile, placid, accommodating himself to conditions, and overtly noncritical of the status quo. The fallacy here tends to rest on the rather universal racial applicability of such features. While some persons may fit any pattern, and all persons fit some pattern, the extent to which patterns of accommodation have been apropos in the case of the Negro in the South is debatable. A more appropriate characterization might be based on the Negro's continuous adjusting and readjusting to the South's never ending development of techniques for reaffirming the subordinate status of the Negro. If there is any one factor that has been constant in Negro-white relations in the South it has probably been the search for effective modus operandi for perpetuating an observed subordinate status for the Negro.

[22] *Ibid.*, pp. 30–35.

If literary depictions have been correct in showing passivity and complacency as characteristic attitudes of Negroes in American society, then perhaps it is not a misnomer to speak of today's Negro as a New Negro. But passivity and complacency have never characterized more than a segment of the Negro population, and no one knows this better than the very keen observers of Negro life familiar with the duality of actions of Negroes. In fact, the Negro has appeared to have a reservoir of reaction patterns ready for release when necessary, but always contingent upon particular situations and circumstances. Thus, each time segments of the Negro group have overtly protested against injustices by fighting back, speaking out, forming militant organizations, or otherwise resisting, they have immediately been given the label "New Negro."

As long as the Negro remained busily engaged in building his own separate institutions and trying to become literate, he was not viewed as a New Negro. Nor was there any attempt to see newness in resistances of Negroes to segregated schools and streetcars. Thus, during the period from 1865 to about 1900, many "New Negro" protests went unnoticed. Several factors were possibly responsible for this, not the least of which was lack of direct and immediate communication between regions. Unlike the televised newscasts of 1967, there were no such ways of showing the Negroes' assault on segregated streetcars in Philadelphia, Pennsylvania, in 1867; in Louisville, Kentucky, in 1871; or the movement of masses of Negroes from the South to Kansas in 1879. Of significance here, however, is the fact that such direct action as was evidenced characterized the Northern, not the Southern, Negro. Yet, in truth, there can be no real separation between these, for migration was the Southern Negro's method of adjusting during this period, while today changing the local situation takes precedence over moving away from the situation as an adjustment technique.

The concept "New Negro" has had both positive and negative connotations and has been used by Negroes themselves, as well as by others. When used by Negroes it has been a technique for developing self-esteem, motivating action, calling attention to changing behavior patterns, or explicitly designating otherwise implicit goals and objectives.

Judging from journalistic attention given to discussions of the New Negro, practically every decade of the twentieth century has witnessed the birth of a New Negro. In 1910, he was portrayed as an educated Negro of the North, whose militancy was mirrored through his NAACP membership. The primary medium of expression for this new militancy was through such Negro periodicals as *Crisis* and *Opportunity*.

In the 1920's, the New Negro was depicted as the young Negro who had become highly race-conscious and who expressed his new race-conscious outlook through the art, poetry and other literary media that were known collectively as the "Harlem Renaissance."[23] Except for age differences, this segment of the New Negro might really be viewed as a mere extension of the existent type of the 1910's. But this in no way completely represented the New Negro, for to some he was a rioter, one whose participation in one of the major riots of 1919 attested to his readiness to fight back. To others, he was a Garveyite, follower of a man whose belief in blackness became a rallying point for unifying the masses. While riots broke out in at least twenty-six American cities in 1919, including Chicago, Washington, and New York, it is significant that all three subtypes of New Negroes—Renaissancer, rioter and Garveyite—were characteristic of New York City. Coexistence of these diverse elements within Harlem itself further substantiates the fact that no single categorization of Negro Americans will suffice and that Negroes' open recognition of their existence probably started destruction of the barriers of antagonism that had stood between the various Negro groups. In addition to this factor, it must be recognized that the outspoken way of evidencing pride and a recognition of beauty in the poetry, song, and blackness previously tabooed as reminiscent of slave status, was itself a manifestation of a spirit fighting to free itself of inferiority feelings and/or inferior statuses.

---

[23] Alain Locke, ed., *The New Negro*.

While the preceding subgroups are indicative of the emergence of several subsidiary New Negro types, all converge, perhaps, when viewing psychologically the spirit of the New Negro
of the 1920's. This was vividly expressed by Du Bois, who, in
depicting the progress of Negro Americans in the five years
preceding 1920, said:

> But above all comes the New Spirit; no longer depending on
> our friends, we are organizing for social uplift and seeking
> alliance with the great national agencies. . . . the mass of
> black folks have made the Great Discovery: they have dis-
> covered each other.[24]

This new discovery, linked with expressed demands for
justice and a new spirit, was well depicted by the editor of the
Black Dispatch, who, in October, 1919, speaking especially to
whites, observed that—

> . . . you now have with you a New Negro . . . not . . . the
> Negro that you have had described to you. You have had
> what was termed a New Negro described to you as an
> insolent, arrogant individual . . . who would not assimilate
> himself properly into organized forms of government. . . .
> out of the education that you have permitted us to get and
> which we have acquired out of our own efforts also, there
> has developed a different creature than the inert clod
> that you once knew as a slave.
>
> . . .
>
> I am alarmed at the idea that some of the people of this
> country have as to the cause of the unrest among us. Others
> say it is Bolshevik or anarchistic influences that seek to
> draw us into their radical division. . . . it does not take
> an I.W.W. to clinch the argument that the majority of
> Negroes in the United States cannot vote. It does not take
> an anarchist to ride with us on the railroad to know that
> when we pay three cents per mile we do not get what you
> get by paying the same identical amount. It does not take

---

[24] *Crisis,* November, 1920.

a Bolshevist to inform us that freedom of movement is restricted to us and that, under the guise of law, a separate status as citizen is designed for the black man.

. . .

None of my race is dreaming of what you so often term "Social Equality."

. . .

What we want is "Social Justice."[25]

Most crucial in affecting the new spirit of the Negro were events and circumstances of the 1930's. By this time, segregation and discrimination had become thoroughly entrenched in the social structure, and many overt manifestations of these phenomena forced upon the Negro an intensive search for self-identity and an extensive search for overt adjustment. Not only were efforts of leadership groups geared to constant emphasis on capitalizing the *n* in *Negro*, but much attention was also given to apprising whites of Negroes' dislike for terms such as nigger, darky, coon; detestation of pickaninny and mammy stories; and resentment over having special socioeconomic factors mentioned as being good for "your people"—emphases similar to those of the 1910's.

Many writings of the 1930's attempt to answer questions relative to the Negro's achieving selfhood. One of the most inclusive views, given in the *Negro Year Book*, takes its clues from the *Amsterdam News:*

> The New Negro, if there is such, is dependent upon himself for his food and thinking; . . . is possessed of a new spirit: believes in self support . . . not only talks 'race pride' but acts it: buys from a Negro grocer, goes to a Negro church, banks with a Negro bank, has insurance with a Negro company. . . . The New Negro is a pioneer for his people . . . refuses to believe he is inferior, though not raising too big a row about it . . . has a new spirit, not necessarily a diploma, a white collar, a salary from charity organizations—he be-

---

[25] Kerlin, *op. cit.*, pp. 63-64.

lieves in God and himself and his future and is hard at work.[26]

This spirit turned inward, concentrating on achieving a Negro selfhood, probably delayed any large-scale overt expressions of general dissatisfaction with existing group status. Contributing to this presumed inactivity was the fact that the New Negro of the 1930's belonged to a middle-class segment in which academic seclusion, intraracial color lines and a "Buy Negro" race-consciousness brought a hopefulness in contradistinction to the hopelessness of the lower classes. Commenting about this group, E. Franklin Frazier noted:

> . . . its main center is Durham (North Carolina). . . . the men are practicing the old-fashioned virtues of the old middle class. . . . in Durham today is a group of colored capitalists who have entered the second generation of business enterprise. . . . the younger generation is building on the foundation of the first generation. . . . [they] have the same outlook of the middle class everywhere. . . .[27]

The attitude of middle-class youth of the 1930's was well described by Reddick. He observed that the black collegians were, prior to 1929, student-council presidents, varsity debaters, and athletic stars in winter, and cuspidor-cleaners and kitchen scullions in summer. Although these jobs were gone after 1929, and student enrollments had dropped, the collegian was still not revolutionary. This lack of revolutionary spirit was attributed to the Negro collegian's being a middle-class American, a respectable bourgeois infected with petty capitalist hopes, aspiring to be like his white-collar parents.[28] It is this, no doubt, that distinguishes the Negro college generation of the 1960's, which tends to be middle class mainly by income and occupational aspirations, rather than by family background. Of interest in regard to the

---

26 Monroe Work, ed., *Negro Year Book*, 1931–32, pp. 16–20.

27 E. Frankin Frazier, "Durham: Capital of the Black Middle Class," Alain Locke, ed., *The New Negro*, pp. 333–340.

28 Lawrence D. Reddick, "What Does the Younger Negro Think?" *Opportunity*, October, 1933, p. 312.

emerging middle classes mentioned here is the fact that they were primarily confined to the South.

By the arrival of the 1940's, the Southern Negro seemed to have resorted to steadily working for equality within the biracial pattern. Simultaneously, however, incidents of protest were developing, although the larger society failed to notice them or considered them of little consequence. Little attention was given to the emergence of a New Negro until the end of the decade. The middle-class Negro had become by now an intraracial "organization man," while the uneducated evidenced passivity and complacency. Factionalism crippled efforts at cooperation between intraracial groups; no one person could speak for the Negro, for functional leaders had long since replaced many earlier types. With the decline of Garveyism, the masses seemed to have become increasingly involved in cult followerships, and persons like Father Divine and Daddy Grace, who had claimed the attention of the masses in the 1930's, managed to hold it in the 1940's.

The circumstances of the 1940's—military, economic, and social—helped speed changes in the cultural levels of Negroes. Having spent the 1930's building faith in legalistic principles and relying on such organizations as the NAACP and Urban League to substantiate this faith, the Negro, in the 1940's, turned to building organizational power bases which were to become the supportive agencies for later protests against injustices. Many of these protests were already under way in the 1940's, especially those involving segregated education, the organized attack on which began in the 1930's, when the NAACP employed a full-time lawyer in its legal department.

The 1940's also saw Negroes fighting against discrimination in the Armed Services, in travel, employment practices, voting, etc. Although many Negroes were beaten, jailed, or even lynched as a result of individual protests in these areas, the 1940's seem to have brought a more profound turning point than ever before in the thinking and actions of Negroes regarding their inequality in status. In the North, a New Negro had fully emerged from experiences of the 1920's and 1930's. World War II was proclaimed a second Civil War and out of it came another New Negro—the classes and masses marching together, no longer rendered powerless by dividing color lines. There was picketing in support of the principle of not buying where you can't work, but primarily, marching in Chicago and Harlem.[29] The Southern Negro was presumed not to have learned even then the technique of direct nonviolent social action.[30] If, however, he was still ignorant of such techniques at the end of World War II, he must be given credit for having hastily mastered these once he began learning them, for violent social action has tended to characterize the northern pattern more than the southern.

Thus, the onset of the 1950's saw greater numbers of Negroes declaring war on their old "give the laws a chance to work" attitude and calling for the immediate cessation of separation and inequality. To hasten the end to inequality by 1963, centennial year of the signing of the Emancipation Proclamation, became the avowed goal, and was issued as such through an NAACP convention in 1953. The May 17, 1954, decision of the Supreme Court outlawing segregation in schools brought a ray of hope to the fight to end inequality. Just as hastily, however, southern states devised delaying tactics with legal sanctions to evade implementation of the Supreme Court decision, and once again a "wait and see" attitude seemed to slow up the quality-seeking actions of Negroes. Even though many groups in various communities were constantly at work knocking bricks out of the slowly tumbling wall of segregation, there was little occupation with depicting a New Negro.

Whites who were suddenly found portraying the existence of the New Negro of the 1960's were apparently indifferent to, unaware of, or unattuned to the many isolated individual and group reactions to racial injustices of the 1940's and 1950's. In similar vein, the Negro himself, after the 1930's, apparently assumed that no further rebirth was being evidenced among Negroes. It seems a valid conclusion to state that the con-

---

29 Adam Clayton Powell, *Marching Blacks*, pp. 46–57.
30 *Ibid.*, p. 115.

ceptualized New Negro, whatever his assumed traits, has been continually emerging since the Civil War, though, in reality, the protesting, direct-action Negro is only newer numerically and classwise than previous New Negro types. The emergent type was emphasized particularly by Negroes themselves up through the 1930's. The literature of the early 1940's and 1950's was relatively silent about such emergence, while interest in the New Negro was revived in the 1960's, being most often emphasized in the latter years by non-Negroes. The delineations mentioned subsequently by decades are but indicators of the changing nature of race relations in an area where change is being continually motivated through direct action—the South.

PART TWO

New Leadership

Much of the literature dealing with today's Negro American is given to discussing the emergence of a new type of Negro leader. Some have sought to give historical perspective to trends in Negro leadership, while a few portray typologies in leadership. Still others have been engaged in reevaluating Booker T. Washington and W. E. B. Du Bois as minority-group leaders. The central problem in all of these studies seems to rest upon determining who the leaders are or have been, for while many have been called "Negro leaders," leadership designation has not necessarily been congruent with Negro acceptance of same.

Leadership has been defined in numerous ways and varied criteria used for locating leaders in the social structure. Frequently, definitions and criteria have been interrelated. Viewing leadership as "the initiation of structure in interaction," Hemphill decrees that when one member of a group initiates actions to which other members react by acquiescence, then the former structures the interaction and sets a difference between his position and that of other group members.[1] Equally significant are two other definitions which involve reciprocal relationships. One states that "leadership is a process of mutual stimulation which, by the successful interplay of relevant individual differences, controls human energy in pursuit of a common cause."[2] The other describes leadership as an interaction between members of a group in which being face-to-face is a *usual* but not

---

[1] Ralph M. Stogdill, *Individual Behavior and Group Achievement,* p. 122.

[2] Sidney Verba, *Small Groups and Political Behavior: A Study in Leadership,* p. 118.

necessary condition. Leadership and followership are, in this instance and to some extent, the same process.[3]

There is, perhaps, no area in which the interaction processes have been more evident than in the civil rights movement. The prevailing process that has characterized the movement has been conflict, the leadership having been born out of inter-racial conflict and sustained through intraracial organizational conflict. While the criteria for designating leaders have been many—personal accomplishments, position or status, group esteem, influence, power, decision-making, and the like—even these, in their operative state, have often generated conflict. Evidence of this is readily observed in the functional leadership of the movement.

Avoiding recapitulation of the many arguments about the leadership of Frederick Douglass, Booker T. Washington, or W. E. B. Du Bois, we may confine our observations to current leadership features. Any attempt to deal with such a fragmented leadership as that existing at present, except by case study, can only magnify the type of dilemma which Robert Penn Warren encountered. He managed to handle the dilemma by distinguishing between a peripheral and a "big brass" leadership, but whether or not he has really located these in terms of follower-ship priorities is still a moot question. According to Warren, the "big brass" include Adam Clayton Powell, Roy Wilkins, Whitney Young, James Forman, James Farmer, Martin Luther King, Bayard Rustin, and the Reverends Abernathy, Shuttlesworth, Wyatt Tee Walker, and Andrew Young. At the periphery, he placed such persons as Hastie, Baldwin, Rowan, Kenneth Clark, and Ralph Ellison.[4] Since his writing, several others have come to the forefront. Even from a functional standpoint, many of these can only be designated leaders of the civil rights movement with respect to their positions or editorializing, for they

[3] Bernard M. Bass, *Leadership Psychology and Organizational Behavior,* p. 89.

[4] Robert Penn Warren, *Who Speaks For The Negro,* Chapters 3 and 4.

are not interacting with any group following. Verbalizing and office-holding are not identical with leadership.

Leadership circles tend to be potentially unlimited, but in a very practical sense, they are confined to local communities. A recent study of the Negro community of Montgomery, Alabama, pointed this up rather sharply. Preliminary analysis of the data indicate that the Montgomery Negro is not particularly leadership-conscious. When asked to name the local Negro leaders, 50.8 per cent of a random sample of 476 respondents named none. Not only did they say that they could not think of any, but they also averred that they did not deal with leaders. Ironically or not, when given a list of names of persons to identify, many of the nationally known personages were more readily identified than were the more locally active ones. Among those respondents who named local leaders, there was wide variation in the individuation of names given but more consensus regarding Martin Luther King as national leader, for 83.0 per cent of the respondents designated him thus. It is highly possible that the Montgomery Negro's rating of Martin Luther King refers back to the bus boycott of 1955–56, which catapulted King into leadership prominence.

Especially significant as a part of the "New Negro" leadership processes in the South is the fact that the leadership is indigenous to the region. While the South has always had its Caucasian-designated Negro leaders in specific communities, it has not always produced leaders who gained national, as well as local, recognition. Nor has it always produced leaders whose self-images were congruent with those of the people they were to lead. Herein may lie much of the success of the social action developed in conjunction with the civil rights movement. At the outset, the movement was functionally middle class, and those who viewed Martin Luther King as the symbolic leader of the movement were assuredly accepting one whose self-image was born of middle-class characteristics. As the movement has become two-pronged, with the masses protesting somewhat differently than did the middle class, new mass-leadership has tended to spring from the working class. A major pertinent change can be noted in the Negro's recognition of leaders acceptable to him, with whom he is willing to cooperate. Rejection of Caucasian-designated leaders tended to make for alienation between leaders and potential followers, and the concomitant development of noncooperation and consensus. If Kelly Miller was correct in asserting that true leadership must be autochthonous,[5] then, as long as leaders emerge from the midst of those to be led, some form of action will be sustained, even through conflict between the leaders themselves. Illustrative of this is the present conflict between leaders over the abandonment of nonviolent tactics in the civil rights movement. Changing self-images of newer leaders, and images they hope to develop in their followers, are probably the master keys to the changing nature of the civil rights movement.

Still another feature of Southern leadership today is the relative absence of those whose lives have been devoid of racial strain. Many of the early leaders, though born in the South, were insulated against numerous forms of segregation that more recent leaders have been forced to endure. Caucasian ancestry, economically secure families, foreign travel, philanthropic aid, and attendance at northern schools tended to serve as the insulators. As these insulators have vanished, attitudes toward them have changed, and the lower socioeconomic classes have become more upwardly mobile; the new leader has become one whose experiences with a closed or segregated society have been more real than vicarious.

Also significant is the fact that organized agencies began to replace individuals as leaders. Starting about 1910 with the NAACP and Urban League, by the 1930's colleges, churches, interracial commissions and the like had taken over the functional leadership. Conflict and social distance between organizations, especially Greek letter ones, tended to hinder development of concerted organizational action. Many of the facets of life now of concern to social action groups formed phases of the national programs of sororities and fraternities. Included among

[5] Kelly Miller, *The Everlasting Strain*, p. 75.

these were such things as encouraging better Negro business, vocational guidance for secondary-school students, book donations for libraries, and scholarship aid to high school and college students.

As worthy as these programs were, they were too meagerly financed, intermittently supported, and selectively oriented to benefit large numbers of Negroes. They failed to reach those outside of school and most in need of assistance. Conflict between the groups at both national and local levels kept the organizations before an intellectual, college-minded public but destroyed the possibility of collective action sufficiently extensive to exert influence outside their own aristocratic inner circles. Yet, during the thirties and forties, groups such as these were the actual leaders rather than specific persons. Walter White, for example, gained recognition among Southern Negroes as an NAACP executive, and not as a result of personal leadership factors. To many, even in the South from which he came, he, like Wilkins, was just a name. In time, however, as such persons have made frequent appearances in local southern communities, identification by a name has been replaced by interaction with a person.

Among the views posited by many writers about the Negro American is one that proclaims today's Negro leadership to be of a new type, characterized by a new militancy that has made the old accommodation type of leader passé. Some have developed typologies of Negro leadership, but only a few basic differences in typologies have really emerged. Following Weber, many early writers classified Negro leaders as traditional, revolutionary, or charismatic. Kelly Miller portrayed two hostile camps of Negro leadership prior to World War I—the quiescent and the assertive.[6]

Less dichotomous is the descriptive characterization of Negro leaders as being nationalistic, i.e., imbued with a militant sentiment of racial pride and solidarity, but differing in degrees of nationalism. Such is the depiction of Standing who, in the 1930's, linked his classifications with historic periods and designated

---

[6] *Ibid.*

schools of leadership which embrace these: (1) Incidental nationalists—the clergy—whose contribution to Negro nationalism was the establishment of a separate Negro society that aided in preparing the way for a nationalistic movement; (2) Militant nationalists who, though following Booker T. Washington's program of racial advancement, were more uncompromising than he on the race problem; (3) The militantly aggressive "talented tenth" of the Du Bois school—mixed-blood residents of the North, whose nationalism rationalized their own social positions; (4) Newer radicals, whose nationalistic motive, combined with mass appeal, made for two subsidiary groups—one demanding unconditional equality and the other substituting "black standards" for white ones.[7]

Declaring that differentiation of the Negro into socioeconomic classes lacking in cohesion hinders the development of a truly race-wide leadership, Guy Johnson classified Negro leaders as gradualists or radicals.[8] He located the first type among Negro professionals and academicians in the South and the latter among younger Negro intellectuals, yet indicated that no race-wide Negro leader could be expected until the intraracial movement built a foundation among the masses.

More recent writings have tended to pattern their classifications after Myrdal, who distinguished between accommodation and protest leaders. Distinctions between pure protest, compromise, and organized-protest leadership, based on types of strategy utilized, indicate variations in these forms of leadership in the South as against the North.[9] Killian and Grigg use an application of the Myrdal thesis and quickly point toward a shift from the old accommodation type of leader to a new protest type, symbolized in the race man who is becoming spokesman for the Negro. They note further that the new protest leader

---

[7] T. G. Standing, "Nationalism in Negro Leadership," *American Journal of Sociology*, XL, No. 2 (September, 1934), pp. 180-192.

[8] Guy Johnson, "Negro Racial Movements and Leadership in the United States," *American Journal of Sociology*, XLIII, (July, 1937), pp. 57-71.

[9] Arnold Rose, *The Negro in America: Condensed Version of An American Dilemma*, Chapter 15.

keeps the Negro community militant through meetings, formal demonstrations, requests, boycotts, lawsuits, and voting.[10] Lomax divides Negro leaders into two factions—militants and dociles. The militants, northern Negroes, are credited with having built the platform upon which the civil rights movement rests, while the dociles—southern Negroes—are defined as the tacticians and decision-makers.[11] Thompson identifies several segments of leaders in the Negro community, viewing these along occupational and racial lines and distinguishing between the Uncle Tom, racial-diplomat, and race-man types.[12]

A study of the 1940's by Drake and Cayton emphasized the role of the race man and race hero as acceptable or radical leadership-types. Acceptable leaders, those who speak for the race and interpret the needs of the community, are considered by whites to be "safe" leaders. The radicals are assumed by the whites to be agitators. Except for changes in names and details, they noted that Bronzeville in 1961 had the same kind of orientation to race men and hero leaders as in the 1940's. Especially noteworthy is the lack of any monolithic unity among leaders and the presence of diverse competing leaders who stimulate each other in their efforts to win gains for Negroes in Bronzeville.[13] Such factors as these have been most characteristic of the South. In the South, where individualized personal relations between Negroes and whites have been coexistent with legalized group-relations, monolithic leadership has been difficult to achieve.

The majority of typologies with regard to Negro leadership appear to be little more than variations on a theme of gradualism, or accommodation; protest, or revolution. The most sociologically relevant typology appears to revolve around designations of functional leaders, differentiated along lines of diverse community interests. Frazier observed that functional leadership

10 Lewis M. Killian and Charles Grigg, *Racial Crisis in America.*
11 Louis E. Lomax, *The Negro Revolt*, p. 43.
12 Daniel Thompson, *The Negro Leadership Class.*
13 St. Clair Drake and Horace Cayton, *Black Metropolis.*

became imperative as the Negro acquired education and developed diverse economic and cultural interests, with the attendant result that no one person could speak for the Negro.[14] In actuality, acceptance of just one or two spokesmen for the Negro has always been more of a white than Negro recognition. Even when Booker T. Washington was declared spokesman, he spoke primarily for an inarticulate proletariat and was more of an interpreter, or liaison, between the races than leader of all Negroes. Any claim for a Du Bois leadership must likewise be seen functionally, for he was in reality a protest editorialist, or propagandist, for the intelligentsia.

Not even Martin Luther King, who has worked full time in the civil rights movement, should be dubbed "the leader" or "the spokesman" for Negroes, for he is merely one of a corps of functional leaders. He may have received more national recognition than many others, but many local persons have been the prime movers in the movement's activities at the community level. Except from an inspirational or symbolic standpoint, many communities have operated free of the influence of King in social action. He has been more operative in the deep South and in the urban ghettoes of the North than elsewhere. Those North Carolina towns, for example, that made headline news because of the 1960 sit-ins now go unheralded, yet many are quietly grappling with problems that have become the foci of the civil rights movement.

The first truly national Negro leadership began to emerge in the 1950's. Such a leadership, however, was only national in terms of its acceptability to large numbers of Negroes dispersed throughout the United States. Most representative of this national leadership has been Martin Luther King, whose local community leadership quickly led to a more or less nationally distributed followership. Few other persons fall in this category, although many writers have dared place them in it. Some persons who were emerging simultaneously with King have since traded their civil rights leadership-roles for others.

---

[14] E. Franklin Frazier, *The Negro in the United States*, Chapter 21.

A few recently named leaders of specific groups have become nationally newsworthy, but their being extensively acceptable national leaders is questionable—except for their acceptance by a nucleus of violence-oriented persons in search of phenomena through which to displace their hatreds and fears.

Meanwhile, conflicts between those heading major civil rights groups have tended to erase the previously existent horizontal leaderships and to establish a hierarchy of vertical leaderships. While the base of the pyramided leadership hierarchy gives little evidence of broadening, its apex is getting precipitously sharp as the ideological distance between leaders lengthens. Instead of the "many small torchbearers showing the way on innumerable fronts," as Cox envisioned Negro leaders,[15] many current leaders seem to be trying to solidify all fronts under a monolithic "black power" structure. The new "black power" leaders may persist in their struggle for survival, but their existence must necessarily be short-lived, for they not only infuriate large numbers of sympathetic whites but are at odds with many Negro leaders and laymen. They make little pretense at being specialists in antagonistic cooperation nor do they invoke the good will of whites—features which, according to Cox, must be a part of race leadership.[16] Their nationalistic aggression will eventually destroy the very structure they seek to erect, for the groups most addicted to "black power" may create many Watts-like situations but the great majority of Negroes living outside Watts-like communities are not likely to succumb to Wattsian influence. This is true particularly of the South.

---

15 Oliver C. Cox, *Caste, Class and Race.*
16 *Ibid.*

PART THREE

Civil Rights: A Continuous Movement

The Negro's aggressive search for equality and freedom is substantively called the civil rights movement, and tactically, a protest movement. Since the former label emphasizes goal, or objective, and the latter, technique, both are perhaps correct. Recent pursuit of differentiated goals by the varied national organizations of Negroes, including SNCC's boycotting and ACT's picketing of the Civil Rights Conference called at the White House for June 1, 1966, suggests that not one but several movements coexist among Negroes. In essence, however, the situation is merely a reflection of an ever present trend among the nation's twenty million Negroes—many specific groups pursuing the same long-range goals but differing in their short-range goals or in methods of achieving both types of goals. It is our thesis that the pursuit of civil rights has been a continuous, not intermittent, movement involving general and localized phases, which have changed as the constituency involved in protest has changed and the problems evoking protest altered or became less acute. The number, national appeal, and life span of the specific phases have tended to vary by regions, as will be noted in the delineations which follow.

The point of origin for a general civil rights movement must be placed at the end of the Civil War, but localized movements in specific communities preceded the Civil War. Especially significant and pertinent in this context have been the shifts in regional emphases and goals of the elite versus the mass of Negroes—a cleavage that is still evident today.

A quasi-separatist movement characterized the post–American Revolution period, for this was the time when Free Negroes of the North sought to build separate churches. Motivated by antagonism and opposition that developed in the racially mixed churches, Negroes tried to achieve equality within a dual social system by building their own parallel institutions. Confinement of this movement to the North was partially a result of restrictions placed on the Free Negro in the South.

The years 1800 to 1831 can be designated as the period of insurrectionary movements in the South—those with which only a few names are usually connected; numerous uprisings were attempted, failing, however, in achievement of desired goals. As this movement declined, the convention movement began to gain momentum in the North. Although the general objective of the convention movement was to improve the status of all Negroes, it did not assume a truly national character until it neared its end in 1869. Numerous forces set in motion following the Civil War probably accounted for the waning of the convention movement. Not the least of these were lack of consensus among followers, shifting orientations of leaders, and the divided interests of Frederick Douglass, who had become the movement's leader and spokesman. For a century or more, social movements among Negroes made frequent shifts along regional lines. Voluntary separation, institutionalization, heightened intragroup communication and education were the characteristic features of these shifting movements.

The years 1865–95 were marked by a waning interest of whites in problems facing the Negro and an increased interest in self-improvement among southern Negroes. These found expression in the development of industrial education, erection of denominational schools, training of ministers to help educate the masses, and migration to the city and to the North. Booker T. Washington's Atlanta speech in 1895 not only influenced the thinking of the period but also supplied answers for questioning whites, indicating how it was possible to build separate Negro and white worlds and yet help Negroes at the same time. By 1900, the Hampton-Tuskegee movement for dignifying labor and developing Negro business tended to commit the Negro community to an economy geared to agricultural pursuits, small business, vocational training, and a philanthropic philosophy undergirded by the Booker T. Washington "separate as the fingers" thesis. Although the movement started in the South, it gained national support and recognition, while concurrently establishing lines of cleavage that prompted many Negroes of the North to start contradictory movements. Descriptive portrayals of the varied movements from 1895 on give some idea of the lines of continuity pervading them, as well as the points of variance among them.

THE HAMPTON-TUSKEGEE PHASE

The first significant Negro movement to develop after the Civil War was the Hampton-Tuskegee movement, which resulted in Booker T. Washington's founding of Tuskegee Institute in 1881. In its origin Tuskegee was little more than a replica of the Hampton Idea, whose influence on Washington was readily discernible, a result of his years of study at Hampton Institute. It was not accident but conscious selection that led the Hampton officials to recommend Mr. Washington to those from the Tuskegee area who wrote to Hampton asking for the name of a person who might be secured as a teacher for the area. And the same conscious selection years later brought Moton, also schooled at Hampton, to succeed Washington.

The industrial-education ideology, on which the Hampton-Tuskegee movement was based, resulted not only in the establishment of an educational center through which it became functional but also in the creation of agencies that helped give the appearance of a contented Negro world. One such agency was the Negro Business League, organized to help foster Negro business. Since industrial education and small, noncompetitive Negro businesses opened avenues for many whites to assist Negroes without fear of losing caste, the lack of interest in the Negro and his problems that had been so apparent after the

Civil War turned into a continuing fund for philanthropic ges-
tures. The Negro Business League, industrial education, rural-
school supervision, organized farm groups, and philanthropic
aid were all so highly concentrated under the direction of one
person that the Hampton-Tuskegee movement began early to
assume institutionalized features.

Perhaps unfortunate in this development was the contingency
of these factors on a power structure reigned over by a single
personality whom whites throughout the nation recognized as
the spokesman for Negroes and the connoisseur of Negro affairs.
Not only did many Negroes for whom Washington could not
speak originate movements in opposition to the Tuskegee Idea
but the movement began to be threatened by the mass migration
of Negroes northward, broadened educational opportunities,
development of many functional leaders among Negroes, and a
militant Negro press addressing itself to racial equality. Among
the assets to be listed creditwise in the ledger of the Tuskegee
Idea are the large numbers of persons trained—even along industrial and agricultural lines—thereby enhancing their potential employability and an educational heritage that continued to
offer training in many occupational areas which, prior to Office
of Economic Opportunity developments of the 1960's, Negroes
were evading. To build and perpetuate such a center, in an area
where not even the school principal could be educationally mobile without having a white person go ahead of him and make
all of his appointments, was in itself quite a feat. Yet, this was
exactly the role played by Mr. Thrasher in conjunction with
Mr. Washington.[1] Debitwise, however, the Tuskegee Idea must
be credited with delaying the Negro's push for a desegregated
society in which the same job opportunities are open to both
Negroes and whites with the same level of training and
competence.

---

[1] Personal document. Information from a Tuskegee citizen who first
went to live in Tuskegee in 1901.

OPPOSITIONAL PHASES

Not only was the Tuskegee Idea criticized by Negro intellectuals almost from its inception, but formal protestations by Negroes of the North resulted in numerous oppositional movements. Significant among the conveyors of opposition were *The Guardian*, a newspaper started by Monroe Trotter in 1901; *The Souls of Black Folk*, a compilation of essays authored by W. E. B. Du Bois in 1903; the Niagara Movement, organized in 1905 as an aggressive actor against post-Reconstruction racial practices; and *Crisis*, journalistic voice of the NAACP, whose publication began in 1910. Editored by Du Bois, *Crisis* continually evidenced the hostility of the northern Negro toward restrictions levied against Negroes and their citizenship rights. Thus, direct agitation through protest literature was the mark of the era.

The Niagara Movement was forerunner of the NAACP which, founded in 1909, became the major counteracting agency against the Tuskegee Idea and thereby symbolized the stand for higher education versus industrial education. Formation of such an organization in 1909 was as daring a venture then as is the establishment of many of the forces opposing it today. The reality of this is very vividly portrayed by one of the charter members of the NAACP, who observed:

> . . . when the Association was formed there were many colored people who believed in the principles for which it stood, who hesitated or refused to join it because they feared membership in it would cause them to lose their jobs or hurt their influence in the communities in which they lived.[2]

After waging its first major court battle in 1915—testing the constitutionality of the grandfather laws—as the 1920 era neared, the NAACP had become sufficiently institutionalized to coordinate its efforts as a pressure group. In the 1920's and 1930's, the NAACP was continuously involved in litigation that would

---

[2] Mary Church Terrell, *A Colored Woman in a White World*, p. 195.

assure the Negro's right to vote in Democratic primaries, give him representation on southern juries, denounce residential segregation, and question the system of public education by race. The organized attack on segregated education, which became a leading NAACP trademark, started in the 1930's, when Charles H. Houston became the first full-time lawyer to head the legal department of the NAACP.[3]

Thus, this major organization fighting for the rights of Negroes began to alter the face of its action-motivated protests. Membershipwise, however, it continued to comprise predominantly the Negro intellectuals. Its failure to appeal to the masses tended to be one of its persistent limitations, at least up until the 1940's. NAACP leaders may be correct in considering the masses as being represented among the organization's current four hundred forty thousand dues-payers,[4] but impersonalized dues-paying bears no necessary relationship to personal participation in activities of the group. Moreover, only in recent years can claims be made for its mass membership, for, as Weyl notes, the NAACP appealed to "colored intellectuals," its membership in 1938 including one-third of the 5,512 "colored college graduates."[5] Its attraction for the masses began to be somewhat in evidence in the 1940's, by which time a membership roll of eighty-five thousand had developed.

For half a century the NAACP was the one formal group which Negroes viewed as their deliverer, but this messianic hope persisted more among the middle classes than among others. Failure of the lower classes to identify with the NAACP can perhaps be traced to its middle-class origin, orientation, and leadership. Even though NAACP verbal proclamations were presumed to be in the interest of all Negroes, for a long while they really spoke for "the talented tenth" interested in *Crisis'* presentations of issues of the day, personal accomplishments, scholarship-winners, book reviews, etc., for the readers of *Souls*

---

[3] Walter White, *A Man Called White*, p. 143.

[4] John K. Jessup, "An Urgent New Reach to Be Equal," *Life*, June 3, 1966, pp. 88–101.

[5] Nathaniel Weyl, *The Negro in American Civilization*, p. 121.

of Black Folk, for the members of college chapters of NAACP, or for the joiners but non-participators. The situation was not even altered significantly by the development of a second organization, the Urban League, which group, with its journal, *Opportunity,* addressed itself to the problems of adjustment of Negro migrants to cities. This would seem to have given the League a lower-class encompassment, but one has only to leaf through *Crisis* and *Opportunity* for the twenties and thirties to note that the same top-level inner circle dominated both the NAACP and the Urban League.

The North remained the center of such movements for an extended period of time, but class lines began to become more and more evident as new movements were engendered. As the elite continued to pursue their goals through NAACP-*Crisis* tactics, the masses evidenced their dissidence by becoming Garveyites. From 1916 to 1927, the Garvey movement, with its race-conscious tenet of blackness and an independent black nation, built up a following among the masses but remained a Northern movement, for it attracted few followers in the South. Although the Garvey movement began in 1914, its most profound influence tended to be felt after World War I ended.

THE GARVEYISTIC PHASE

The Universal Improvement Association (UNIA), established by Marcus Garvey in his Jamaican home town, started out to be a replicated Tuskegee movement extended to Jamaica. Imbued with the Booker T. Washington philosophy of industrial education, Garvey hoped to visit Tuskegee, embark on a speaking tour through the southern United States, and seek counsel from Washington on securing philanthropic support for establishing prototype Tuskegees in the West Indies.[6] Many situational factors seem to have made Negroes in the U.S. more likely adherents to Garveyism than Jamaicans. Not only was

---

[6] Edmund David Cronon, *Black Moses,* pp. 4–20.

Washington's reaction to Garvey's proposed visit coolly non-committal, but he died before Garvey was able to make the trip to the United States. Nor were West Indians interested in such educational and industrial schools. After working and observing the status of Negroes in parts of Europe and Central and South America and declaring his intentions of becoming a race leader, Garvey made the objectives of UNIA those of universal brotherhood. He hoped to achieve this through the concerted action of Negro people throughout the world, the focus for which became blackness as a symbol of national greatness. Jamaicans had no reason for being attracted to this idea, for the West Indian social structure was based upon color-caste divisions.

Recognizing the hostility of Jamaican mulattoes and the indifference of the blacks to his idea of racial redemption, Garvey sought to determine whether or not American Negroes would accept his views. He arrived in Harlem in March, 1916, to test the reception of his ideas. While there was no immediate indication of the success he might expect with his program of Black Nationalism, by 1917 he had begun to amass a large number of followers. All evidence points to the fact that Garveyism remained a vital influence in the lives of the Negro masses of northern urban centers from 1917 to 1927. Extending the original program into a Back-to-Africa Movement and spending the first few years in preparation for building an independent African nation, UNIA tended to become an all-encompassing organization with a self-sufficient economic base. A Negro factories corporation that opened up many small businesses, and a steamship company proposed as the commercial link between Negro peoples of the world, became the major ventures through which resources and materials were to be secured to implement the Back-to-Africa Movement.[7]

UNIA structure comprised a parent organization with headquarters in New York City and local branches in other cities. Each member was assessed a monthly fee, the larger portion of which went to the local division and the smaller, to the parent

[7] *Ibid.*, pp. 51-61.

body.[8] Modeling the organization after fraternal orders that gave sickness and death benefits was thought to be a good drawing card for securing memberships among the masses, but apparently financial adequacy in this area was never really obtained. Although the movement failed to attract the Negro bourgeoisie and had to reinterpret its black-skin symbol in the light of the polyglot American Negro population, it appears to have had quite an impact on the Negro's developing self-esteem. Appeal also came through annual conventions, recognition through titles, colorful parades, ostentatious uniforms, and propaganda in the movement's paper, the *Negro World,* a weekly published from 1918 to 1933.

Just as groups of middle-class Negroes criticized the Tuskegee movement almost from its inception, so, too, was Garveyism criticized. Garveyism became a movement of the masses, for it offered them a foreseeable future in which they believed they could change the northern situation of inequality, about which they had been so thoroughly disillusioned before migrating from the South. As their belief in Garveyism began to be strengthened, it became difficult to eradicate this through criticisms of the movement and its leader. However, when Garvey was deported in 1928, after having been incarcerated in the federal prison in Atlanta, charged with having used the U.S. mails to defraud, UNIA began to decline. While Garvey envisioned continuing the movement in other parts of the world, it never seemed to have the same appeal that it had had in the U.S. It is highly probable that these same security-seeking masses of the twenties and thirties helped spark the opening for the Father Divine and Daddy Grace movements that became so popular during this time, though their philosophy and structure differed. A major difference between these early Negro movements and later ones is that they were so single-leader dominated that removal of the leader from the scene almost spelled death for the movement.

As the NAACP and Garveyism continued apace in their de-

---

[8] *Ibid.*

velopment, other movements began to come into existence. The 1918–19 period witnessed the onset of a renaissance among both the elite and the masses of Negroes in the North. Among the masses, militancy began to be expressed through riots, while militancy of the elite showed in the art and writings of a group of intellectuals who sought to enhance the self-respect of Negroes by glorifying their accomplishments. It is difficult to assess the influence of the Garveyist-inclined masses on the race-conscious views and attitudes of the elite. Perhaps it simply took time for the Negro to reach a point where, two generations removed from slavery, he could feel comfortable with, and unashamed of, his identifying racial characteristics as emphasized by social definition.

INTERRACIAL PHASES

Coexistent with these was a pluralistic interracial movement that got under way early in the twentieth century. Even though no consciously intentional efforts motivated the development of a general interracial movement—which started early in the 1900's and became differentiated into several specific movements extending through the 1940's—historical circumstances seem to support the contention that such an entity existed. The branch movements that developed from a central core of interracial concern included the Niagara Movement, the NAACP, the National Urban League, the Race Relations Commission, the National Negro Congress, the Durham Conference, CORE, and the Southern Regional Council. Only one of these, the NNC, remained predominantly intraracial in its following or membership, but even this group had whites in attendance at its 1940 meeting. A principal reason for its intraracial makeup was that it sought to solidify the Negro's struggle for equality by unifying all Negro organizations and gaining support of the masses; however, it only remained in existence for about five years, 1935–40.

Especially interesting and somewhat contradictory was the origin in the South of an interracial group whose aims were to eliminate lynchings and mob violence and secure legal justice for the Negro. Spurred by the establishment in 1919 of a Commission on Interracial Cooperation, the movement was sponsored by a white group and a group of Negroes in the South, given financial support from the North, and committed to educating racial groups through personal contacts at conferences and the like.[9]

Prior to this, Carter G. Woodson and four associates had organized in Chicago, in 1915, a movement for interracial cooperation through knowledge and understanding. Its formal structure was that of an "Association for the Study of Negro Life and History." Hoping to be the liaison in bringing harmony between the races, the Association sought to interpret one race to the other through its *Journal of Negro History*. Additional information reached the public through Negro History Week observances and the publishing of a *Negro History Bulletin,* the latter intended for public schools.

Growth and extension of the race-relations movement can be readily determined from the many interracial departments, councils, and committees attached to churches, YM- and YWCA's religious and labor groups. Operation of this movement within the confines of the South, which by 1920 had a body of segregation laws aimed at restricting interracial contacts, was perhaps destined from the beginning for many superficial accomplishments.

Early phases of the movement made their most profound impact through the NAACP, as previously indicated. Two groups that have become increasingly significant, although different structurally and functionally and separated in time of origin by thirty-one years, must be viewed along with those already mentioned. These are the Urban League and the Congress of Racial Equality (CORE).

Although the National Urban League is considered by many as a major civil rights organization, it must be viewed differently from other organizations with which it is usually compared.

---

[9] Paul E. Baker, *Negro-White Adjustment: An Investigation and Analysis of Methods in the Interracial Movement in the United States.*

Being a social service organization interested in breaking down discriminatory practices in employment, housing, health, family life, etc., would naturally give it a civil-rights base. However, it should not be considered as a direct action organization operating in the civil-rights protest vein along with NAACP, SNCC, CORE, and SCLC. It does not even have a sufficiently dispersed local-league base to warrant being so classified. Since the action program of the Urban League is directed at the fundamental issues that civil rights groups are now recognizing as the real bases from which the movement must stem if lasting gains are to be made, the League may have greater stakes in changes initiated in the future than it has had in those of the past.

Perhaps no group has more of a claim to being interracially based than does CORE, whose first chapters were urban, young adult, middle-class, college-centered, Northern entities, whose action embraced sit-ins and picket lines. The organization began in Chicago in 1942 and spent much of its time in training new members through workshop sessions that sought to instruct the members on how to respond to insults with goodwill. Not until the 1950's did the CORE idea of direct action secure a base in the South, its real fame being a product of the 1960's. As attention began to shift from sit-ins in restaurants and open-occupancy housing to jobs in consumer-oriented industries that were amenable to CORE-type pressures, more workingclass Negroes were drawn into the organization. This, according to Rich, subtly changed the character of the middle-class and predominantly white northern chapters.[10] Then the 1961 Freedom Rides, which were initiated, sponsored, and financed by CORE, took the organization into the hard-core South, where it met some of its most hostile opposition, including the killing of some of its staff members.

In 1942, Southern Negro leaders met in conference at Durham, North Carolina, and proposed another scheme for inter-

---

[10] Marvin Rich, "The Congress of Racial Equality and Its Strategy," *Annals of the American Academy of Political and Social Science*, Vol. 357 (January, 1965), pp. 114–117.

racial cooperation in the South. Equalization of educational opportunites was proffered as the means of eliminating inequalities. Later that same year, at a conference of whites and Negroes called in Atlanta, appeals for educational equality as stressed at Durham were placed before the group, and the Atlanta Conference agreed to cooperate.[11] Efforts of an Atlanta Continuing Committee to implement the intent of the Durham, Atlanta, and later, Richmond, conferences resulted in the formation in 1944 of the Southern Regional Council. The SRC was started as an informational and action organization dedicated to improve economic, civic, and racial conditions in the South through research and interracial dialogue under codirectors—one Negro, the other white.[12] Distortion of the Council's work through political demagoguery, and the South's refusal to meet the challenge of the Durham manifesto or promote the objective purposes of SRC, eradicated the last chances of applying Plessy vs. Ferguson principles to southern education.[13] Hence, the innumerable cases taken to the courts by the NAACP in the 1940's in behalf of Negroes seeking equal educational opportunities. This was followed by the hopeful alertness of the 1950's, while awaiting implementation of the 1954 Supreme Court decision. Then came the point at which the delaying, negating, and noncompliance tactics of southern states and their demagogues forced a shift in the Negro's quest for equality from a movement of conference requests for cooperative action to one of demands for equality by demonstration. A major result of the Council's development was its decentralization in 1954, which culminated in the establishment of "Councils on Human Relations" in southern states. The latter became relatively autonomous about 1957 and left SRC a cooperative body of about one hundred members.[14] Interracial cooperation through contact and dialogue continue to be expressed through the state councils.

---

[11] Thomas D. Clark, *The Emerging South*, p. 184.

[12] The Southern Regional Council, Its Origin and Purpose, Appendix F.

[13] Clark, *op. cit.*, p. 185.

[14] Leslie W. Dunbar, "The Southern Regional Council," *Annals*, Vol. 357 (January, 1965), pp. 108–112.

ADJUNCT MOVEMENTS

Still another movement that developed in the North was the selective-buying campaign of the 1920's and 1930's. Prior to this period, the Negro world consisted predominantly of two classes: freedmen and freemen, or the masses and the elite. The dichotomy in movements of these groups has been pointed out in preceding discussions. By the 1920–30 era, an extended, emergent Negro middle class began to alter the pattern. In this, the Negro American merely recapitulates the history of the American nation and the Western World. Thus, the selective-buying movement of the 1920's and 1930's can be attributed to this middle class, although the movement was confined to the North. The Negro middle class of the South during this period was too busy building its separate world of business, schools, educated children, fraternal and social life, and perpetuating its academic seclusion and its intraracial social status to destroy its handiwork by demanding an openly integrated world. In a manner of speaking, it appears that although the Tuskegee Idea of industrial education had been negated, a "separate as the fingers but united as the hand" economy was being protected. To many, the Negro in the South remained seemingly so passive and insensitive to change during these years that labels of complacency, unconcern, and satisfaction began to follow him. Little did the labelers realize that the Negro in the South was unobtrusively outdistancing the Negro in the North; that he would yet point the way for true emancipation of all Negro Americans; or that the real Yankees to upset the southern pattern would be local Negroes whose experiences with segregation and discrimination had equipped them with emotionally toned reactions to withstand southern whites' opposition.

In analyzing varied movements among Negroes, many writers list the proposed 1941 March on Washington as a major movement. The proposal failed to reach movement status, for it did not materialize. Executive Order 8802, which created FEPC, was designed to offset the March by dealing with issues of discrimination in employment. After its passage, the proposed March on Washington lost support.

The 1940's was the period when the southern middle-class Negro was becoming economically secure, while individually testing and protesting discriminatory practices. Legal attacks had been made in the 1930's against inequalities in school facilities, per capita pupil expenditures, teacher salaries, etc. Subtle protests against discrimination in such areas as public transportation and consumer buying had been engaged in even prior to 1940, but they often went unobserved or were ignored. In the 1940's, the momentum seemed to quicken for using subtlety in protesting, thus setting in motion an undercurrent protest movement that helped hasten the era of overt demonstration which developed after many legal changes provided a basis for insisting on change in numerous areas. This undercurrent protest was evident in risks taken by Negroes in refusals to sit behind "screens" on city buses in the deep South, to move to the rear of streetcars and buses in the upper South, or to sit with other Negroes so that whites might be seated on interstate modes of transportation—all this even before the 1946 law banning segregation in interstate travel or the 1956 decree against segregation on public buses.

While these refusal tactics often resulted in "loud talk" criticism by other Negroes, ejection, beatings, arrests, and sometimes, lynching, they were indicative of an emerging "stand still and fight" attitude of the middle-class Negro. Walter White aptly described the situation by declaring that "a firm resolve came unnoticed into the pattern of Negro thinking and action to end separation and inequality."[15] Not even the many court suits asking for damages and challenging segregated travel facilities served as adequate harbingers of significant mass action by Negroes. In short, the stage was being set for assuming dramatic roles of action after the educational drama reached its climax in 1954—a period which was to be followed by an anticlimax stretched over an ensuing six-year interim.

---

[15] Walter White, *How Far the Promised Land,* p. 168.

There was no way of foreseeing exact developments and out-
comes, but Southern middle-class Negroes of the forties and
fifties could attest to the frequency with which groups and individuals reminded themselves and others that the millennium
was not far distant. The unseen motivators, who perhaps recognized this better than others, were those persons in non-
state-supported colleges who were constantly prodding their
students—and there were many of them—to make certain to
integrate those transportation facilities which had been legally
desegregated. From the standpoint of being aware of such developments, the Negro was a better predictor of collective behavior than was his white neighbor, who labored under the myth
of Negro satisfaction with the status quo. The seventeen-year
fight for admission to many southern colleges, graduate and pro-
fessional schools—from the Hocutt Case of North Carolina (1933)
to the Sweatt Case of Texas (1950) and the McLaurin Case of
Oklahoma (1950)—should have served notice that the Negro was
going to continue to fight for rights that belonged to him.

It is a misnomer to speak of the civil rights movement as
having started in 1960 with the sit-ins. In actuality, this was
merely another generation's overt protest against injustice and
inequality. Moreover, it was simply another phase of a continuous struggle in which Negroes were involved for at least a
century, with each generation protesting differently but developing through historical experience the emotional readiness
upon which reforms thrive—when initiated at the right time,
in the right place, under the right circumstances. Supportive of
this fact are the many types of protests in which Negroes engaged decades before 1960.

Many writers who have undertaken analyses of trends in the
civil rights movement currently seem baffled over whether or
not it really is a movement. This is predicated upon the about-
face made by CORE and SNCC in July, 1966, as they challenged
the ideology and tactics of the movement—nonviolence and
passive resistance—and called for "black power" and retaliation
with violence whenever the Negro finds violence being meted
out to him. The "angry leaders" who initiated this revolutionary

shift have done the same thing that the early sit-iners did when they acted first and planned later. And just as the adult community had to become the financial support for a student population that was without money to buy coffee when the coffee shop opened—or that was itself unaffected by selective buying—so, too, have other organizations had to come to the rescue of those which, even with dwindling resources, are clamoring for black power and the discard of the nonviolent philosophy.

There does seem to be a major difference here, however. The sit-iners were not involved in an ostentatious struggle for leadership that made it mandatory for them to see what strategy they could use for regaining recognition for their organizations, which were being overshadowed by others, as was so in the case of the new CORE and the new SNCC. Whether this grows out of displaced values or frustration born of inaction, as many have claimed, it is difficult to say. The only assured development at this point is that while the movement will continue to live—with even more fervor perhaps—its basic structure has been affected in numerous ways. There is little doubt of continued existence of the serial actions discussed here as a movement, for we take the Abel position that a movement is pluralistic behavior functioning as an organized mass-effort directed toward a change of established folkways or institutions.[16] As a social collective, there may be some question of its being held together by common interests and sentiments if these are viewed specifically; but, generically speaking, the common goals still obtain. The fragmented actions and tactics recently engaged in by SNCC and CORE savor of the extreme nationalism of Garveyism some four decades ago but are less compatible with today's society than was Garveyism with its society.

The "black power" group developing within the civil rights milieu seems on its way to becoming a separate movement, although its aims point toward simply changing the philosophy and tactics of the already established civil rights movement. Its leaders argue that nonviolence is passé and that it is time for

---

[16] Theodore Abel, *Why Hitler Came Into Power*, p. 348.

King to step down and let others take the lead. In actuality, replacement of one group by the other cannot be automatically accomplished. The "black power" group addresses itself to the poverty and misery of the ghetto. It depends on votes, boycotts, and defiance to give the Negro confidence in himself so that he will take control of his own destiny. Even if it succeeds in Harlem, Watts, Vine City, or Lowndes County, it omits a large and continually growing segment of the Negro population, people whose self-image is not mirrored through communities of this type, regardless of what the stereotyped views of others might be.

What the "black power" group really offers is an invitation to racial warfare and interclass conflict. Garveyism spoke to a disillusioned urban populace in the early 1920's and built its promises on a form of "black power," but it failed to attract the Negro bourgeoisie. There is every reason to believe that a "black power" movement will be no more appealing to the Negro bourgeoisie today than it was four decades ago. The exception may be that youthful minority which has become frustrated in its search for upward mobility from the lower to the middle class.

Functionally, the SCLC is rapidly maturing into an organization that may take first place among groups vying for leadership roles in the civil rights struggle. Its organizational structure, planned originally by Bayard Rustin,[17] is not far different from that of other groups whose traditional form calls for a president, vice-president, executive administrator, and the like. However, its six basic programs are functionally more relevant to the civil rights struggle than are the programs of many other traditionally structured organizations. The programs include (1) political education and voter registration; (2) operation breadbasket (job opportunities); (3) direct action; (4) citizenship education; (5) operation dialogue (interracial communication); and (6) nonviolent training, special projects, and fund raising.[18]

---

[17] *Ebony*, June, 1965.
[18] *Ibid.*

The recent decisions to proceed with the remaining Summer 1966 operations in Mississippi—made following the dissonance ensuing from the Meredith Memphis-to-Jackson march—were probably the most timely of decisions and will permit continued vital functioning of the group and retention of its non-violent philosophy. With the leadership of SNCC and CORE clamoring for a "black power" ideology and retaliation through violence, as events of June, 1966, so clearly indicate, any continued coordination of activities of SCLC, SNCC, and CORE will undoubtedly undermine the entire movement—unless SNCC and CORE redirect their thoughts and actions.

It is understandable that impatience should replace patience in areas where freedom marchers have encountered unnecessary violence, as in the states of Alabama and Mississippi. However, for the marchers to retaliate with violence would merely result in further destruction of life and property, continued intimidation and harassment, and the evolution of suppressive legal tactics by those in the power structure whose existing power is already sufficient to make demonstration necessary just to secure compliance with existing laws which grant privileges and rights to all, irrespective of race.

It cannot be rightly claimed that the civil rights movement has left the South and gone North, except for its more overt demonstration-phases. On the one hand, it has simply become diffused throughout the nation. Its focus in the North is on areas where problems are most acute, where fear of movement-sabotage by alienated ghetto rioters has led to the development of planned activity as a control, or where northern Negroes have seen the urgent need for initiating change in their communities lest their southern brothers gain equality first. On the other hand, many southern communities have passed through the stage of protest marching or demonstrating and are now at the bargaining stage, where the conference table is being used. In addition, the very structure of the community may be an important factor in determining the feasibility of sustained disruption of the community through active participation in demonstrations.

In Tuskegee, Alabama, for example, where the middle-class Negro prevails and two institutions—Tuskegee Institute and Veterans Hospital—dominate the socioeconomic structure, extensive participation in demonstrations could disrupt the total community. This is exactly what did transpire early in January, 1966, when a crisis situation developed over the slaying of a Tuskegee Institute student, the occurrence evoking marches and demonstrations that disrupted daily routines. After the first week, a semicalm prevailed, and fewer and fewer people became directly involved in demonstrating, while more and more people took interest in the activities of a newly formed committee which sought to get the city council to pass ordinances that would make it easier to deal with similar situations in the future—if such should occur. Unfortunately, the Committee, functioning as an Ad Hoc Committee for Justice in Alabama, gradually overextended itself and eventually dissolved with the expectation of forming a new structure.

Despite the fact that it was the Negro middle class who initiated the 1960 phase of the civil rights movement, it is inaccurate to state that the movement has been taken over by the masses and by extremist groups. It has simply ceased to be a predominantly middle-class movement and has become splintered, for as the masses have become involved, many new groups or organizations representing their particular interests have come into being. These have not replaced the more solidary organizations, such as NAACP and SCLC, but are additional or supplementary. It does appear, however, that keeping the movement nonviolent has become increasingly difficult as its base has broadened. Even during the 1960 demonstrations in Raleigh, North Carolina, for example, there were numerous occasions when persons from the Third Ward area appeared en masse with weapons and offered protection to the many hundreds of Shaw and St. Augustine's college students who were heckled by whites while staging their downtown marches. To refuse this type of aid and yet maintain the good will of a group whose loyalty would be needed for later phases of the movement became difficult but proved manageable.

At the national level there are five major groups that are usually viewed as comprising the leadership oligarchy of the civil rights movement—NAACP, Urban League, SCLC, CORE, and SNCC. But, at the local level, where direct involvement has been most meaningful, these groups have not always been the most effective. In fact, in many communities alienation between these groups and variations in their respective goals have often made cooperation for action so difficult as to necessitate formation of a new, all-embracing citizens' group. Such a group has often been in a better position to establish its own lines of authority, allocation of funds, and forms of action. Since SCLC had not yet become so highly organized in 1960 and SNCC was not formed until 1960, these organizations were not appreciably affected by this early 1960 organizational divisiveness, but they did undoubtedly feel the impact of later inroads. It is particularly difficult to assess this in the case of SNCC, for though loosely structured and highly fluid, it is completely different in goals, outlook, lines of action, and followership from the SNCC organized in April, 1960, in Raleigh, North Carolina. SNCC's latest move for developing power through an all-Negro party, and its repudiation of whites, would now place it with other black-nationalist groups, especially the Black Muslims.

The new SNCC and some more recently organized groups, ACT (1963), RAM (1964), and Deacons (1965), point toward a rising new movement comprised of those interested in violence. It is hardly conceivable, however, that the more stable middle class will become their followers or that large numbers of persons outside the urban ghettoes of the North will accept their philosophy as a working principle. The leader of ACT, for example, who organizes action cells in slums and likes to criticize VIP's and harass social workers, was expelled from certain civil rights organizations for being too "aggressive, dictatorial, or irresponsible."[19] Such a person will certainly not find it easy to gain a following among those he tries so diligently to anger. What appears imminent is an interclass conflict that will create a lesser movement, one which may well destroy

---

[19] *Ebony,* May, 1965.

and negate much of the previously existent unity, cooperation and solidarity. While complete dissolution of the major civil rights movement does not seem to be in the offing, its reduction to a quasi-movement does, such a movement being one in which large numbers of people "may cooperate in some respects," yet pursue individual objectives.[20] Sentiments may hold it together superficially, but the widening gap between middle- and lower-class Negroes may be expected to be reflected actionwise. Although the movement is middle class in origin, it has gradually attracted the lower class. However, a wedge is now being driven between the two classes as the "black power" militants speak to the impoverished ghettoes. Future developments must inevitably depend upon the nature of Negro leadership.

---

[20] John and Mavis Biesanz, *Modern Society,* p. 103.

Bibliography

Abel, Theodore. *Why Hitler Came Into Power*. New York: Prentice-Hall, Inc., 1938.

Baker, Paul E. *Negro-White Adjustment*. Pittsfield, Mass.: Sun Printing Co., 1934.

Bass, Bernard M. *Leadership, Psychology and Organizational Behavior*. New York: Harper and Row, 1960.

Biesanz, John and Mavis. *Modern Society*. Englewood Cliffs, N.J.: Prentice-Hall, Inc., 1964.

Clark, Thomas D. *The Emerging South*. New York: Oxford University Press, 1961.

Cox, Oliver C. *Caste, Class and Race; A Study in Social Dynamics*. New York: Monthly Review Press, 1959.

Cronon, Edmund David. *Black Moses*. Madison, Wis.: University of Wisconsin Press, 1962.

Drake, St. Clair and Horace Cayton. *Black Metropolis*. New York: Harper Torchbooks, 1962.

Frazier, E. Franklin. *The Negro in the United States*, rev. ed. New York: The Macmillan Co., 1957.

Foner, Philip S. *Life and Writings of Frederick Douglass*. Vol. II. New York: International Publishers Co., Inc., 1950.

Kerlin, Robert. *The Voice of The Negro*. New York: E. P. Dutton and Co., 1919.

Killian, Lewis M. and Charles Grigg. *Racial Crisis in America*. Englewood Cliffs, N.J.: Prentice-Hall, Inc., 1964.

Locke, Alain, ed. *The New Negro*. Albert and Charles Boni, Inc., 1925.

Logan, Rayford W., ed. *What the Negro Wants*. Chapel Hill, N.C.: University of North Carolina Press, 1944.

Lomax, Louis E. *The Negro Revolt*. New York: Harper and Row, 1962.

Miller, Kelly. *The Everlasting Strain*. Washington, D.C.: Associated Publishers, 1924.

Powell, Adam Clayton. *Marching Blacks*. New York: Dial Press, Inc., 1955.

Rose, Arnold. *The Negro in America*. New York: Harper Torchbooks, 1964.

Sterling, Dorothy and Benjamin Quarles. *Lift Every Voice*. Garden City, N.Y.: Doubleday and Co., 1965.

Stogdill, Ralph M. *Individual Behavior and Group Achievement*. New York: Oxford University Press, 1959.

Terrell, Mary Church. *A Colored Woman in a White World*. Ransdell Publishers, 1940.

Thompson, Daniel. *The Negro Leadership Class*. Englewood, N.J.: Prentice-Hall, Inc., 1963.

Toby, Jackson. *Contemporary Society*. New York: John Wiley and Sons, Inc., 1964.

Verba, Sidney. *Small Groups and Political Behavior: A Study in Leadership*. Princeton, N.J.: Princeton University Press, 1961.

Warren, Robert Penn. *Who Speaks for the Negro*. New York: Random House, Inc., 1965.

Weyl, Nathaniel. *The Negro in American Civilization*. Washington, D.C.: Public Affairs Press, 1960.

White, Walter. *A Man Called White*. New York: Viking Press, Inc., 1948.

———. *How Far The Promised Land*. New York: Viking Press, Inc., 1955.

Work, Monroe, ed. *Negro Year Book*, 1916–17, 1918–19, 1931–32.